INCARNATION

INCARNATION

Alister McGrath

Fortress Press

Minneapolis

INCARNATION

First Fortress Press Edition 2006

Scripture quotations are from the New Revised Standard Version of the Bible,
copyright © 1989 by the Division of Christian Education of the National Council
of the Churches of Christ in the USA and used by permission.

Cover art: *Nativity* by Anthony Van Dyck (1599–1641),
Galleria Nazionale d'Arte Antica, Rome, © 1990, Photo Scala,
Florence – courtesy of the Ministero per i Beni e le Attività Culturali.
Cover and interior design and typesetting: Theresa Maynard

ISBN: 0-8006-3701-1

Manufactured in Belgium

10   09   08   07   06   1   2   3   4   5   6   7   8   9   10

contents

introduction

Who is Jesus Christ? And why is he so important? We simply cannot avoid these questions, nor can we evade the need to answer them to ourselves, or to those outside the Church. Why do Christians believe that Jesus of Nazareth holds the key to the mystery of God and of human destiny? Why not some other person? Or some timeless idea, detached from the world of human life and history?

Even in the Gospels, we find Jesus provoking amazement, admiration, bewilderment, even outrage in those who see and hear him. Human minds and tongues have never been fully up to the task of making sense of him. It has proved easier to identify inadequate ways of speaking and thinking about Jesus than to do justice to his words and ways.

So what way of conceiving Jesus is most faithful to the Gospel records? What way of picturing him seems best adapted to safeguard and enfold the complex witness of the New Testament to his impact on people? As the Church wrestled with Jesus of Nazareth, there was a dawning, painful recognition that it was going to be impossible to do full justice to his identity and significance. What is important is to identify what really matters. To *expand* our appreciation of Jesus in worship and in prayer, we need to *limit* our understanding of his identity. We must focus on what seems to be the best way of visualizing his significance and placing him on the complex map charting the relationship of humanity and divinity.

So what is that way? And why is it both important and genuinely helpful to Christians? The answer lies in the title of this volume – *incarnation*. It speaks of God entering into the messy, fallen world that we inhabit. It invites us to think of God opening a window into his being, and a door into his presence. And how does he do this? And when does he do this? The doctrine of the incarnation tells us that it is in and through that remarkable person called 'Jesus of Nazareth'.

Even to those who have become used to the idea through the preaching and liturgy of the Church, it is still startling, possibly even baffling. How can such a statement be made about any historical figure? And how on earth are we to make sense of the seemingly nonsensical statement that we are to think of Jesus as truly divine and truly human? And what difference does it make to the experience and the prayer of Christian people? To appreciate these matters, we must first understand them; and to understand them, we must first believe them.

This book sets out to engage both the believing mind and imagination, by exploring something of what led the Church to set out its faith and hope in this extraordinary, brilliant and bold idea that Jesus Christ is God incarnate. Many books are needed to do justice to this theme; we must limit ourselves to skimming the surface of its vast depths, hopefully encouraging others to go further. In this brief volume, we shall enter into the Gospel narratives, stimulating both our reason and imagination as we reflect on the words and deeds of Jesus of Nazareth, and why they at times painfully yet always inexorably lead us to this deeper conclusion about who he is, and why he matters. And as it is impossible to engage with the Gospels without using the 'sight of our imagination' (Ignatius Loyola), we shall allow a series of images and words, drawn from the wealth of the Christian theological and artistic traditions, to explore both the *truth* and the *reality* of the Christian faith.

Alister McGrath

the fulfilment of prophecy

the fulfilment of prophecy

'Who do people say that I am?' (Mark 8.29). Jesus' question to the disciples retains its power and challenge. The discipleship of the mind that is rightly expected of all Christians invites us all to reconsider our estimation of Jesus. How best can we make sense of him? How can we locate him on a conceptual map? How do we place him along the coordinates of time and eternity, humanity and divinity, particularity and universality? How can an event which took place at a specific time and place be relevant for all people and all times? How on earth are we to make sense of the momentous events packed into a tiny slice of human history that we call 'Jesus of Nazareth' ?

This short book sets out to begin that process of exploration, engaging both the believing imagination and mind. We shall allow the story of Jesus to impact our thinking and imagining. For some, stories have no meaning other than those we choose to impose upon them. Yet there is something different about the Gospel narrative of Jesus. It invites us to set our prejudices and preconceptions to one side, and focus on what the disciples saw and heard – events and actions that they so clearly wanted to pass down to us, so that we might relive their experiences, and share their conclusions.

Yet the story of Jesus of Nazareth is not to be told in isolation. To understand the identity and significance of Jesus, we must tell other stories – stories that interlock and interrelate, setting the context for making sense of the theological puzzle that Jesus himself set his disciples. One of those stories concerns God's creation of the world; another tells of God's calling of Israel; a third tells the age-old human quest for meaning and significance. The story of Jesus intersects all three, ultimately to provide their fulfilment. Jesus is the focal point from which all other stories are to be seen, and on whom all finally and marvellously converge.

This theme has fascinated theologians throughout Christian history, especially those of the Greek-speaking Church of the first five centuries.

The great Egyptian city of Alexandria was noted for its philosophical sophistication. Several schools of thought, all basing their ideas on the great classical philosopher Plato, argued for the existence of an ideal world, lying beyond the world of appearances. But how could this shadowy and elusive realm be known? Or, more tantalizingly, how might it be *entered*? Growing importance came to be attached to the idea of the *logos*, a Greek term best translated as 'word', referring to something – or perhaps someone – that could mediate between these two very different, yet apparently interconnected, worlds. But how might this gap be bridged? Who could bring the ideal realm into the everyday world? Or bring people from the present order of things to the ideal world lying beyond it?

Alexandria was also home to a highly cultured Jewish population, well aware of the importance of the questions raised by Greek philosophy, yet faithful to their own way of seeing the world. For such writers, the concept of law was of critical importance. Law represented God's will, the ultimate standard of life, and the true goal of human nature. Yet many within Judaism knew that the law did not represent the final state of things. It was an interim measure, a staging-post on the way to something still better. Many waited for the fulfilment of the law – for the culmination of the hopes of Israel in God's anointed one, the Messiah. A new prophet was awaited, who would be as Moses, and know God face to face. A new king was expected, who would restore the fortunes of Israel's great monarch David. A new priest would come, in the line of Aaron, who would finally purge the guilt of his people.

Many in Alexandria were waiting for the fulfilment of their hopes. Both Greeks and Jews – the two most prominent people-groups of the New Testament – were longing for their grand dreams to become reality. Their theories were like maps, pointing to an expected, yet still unknown, city

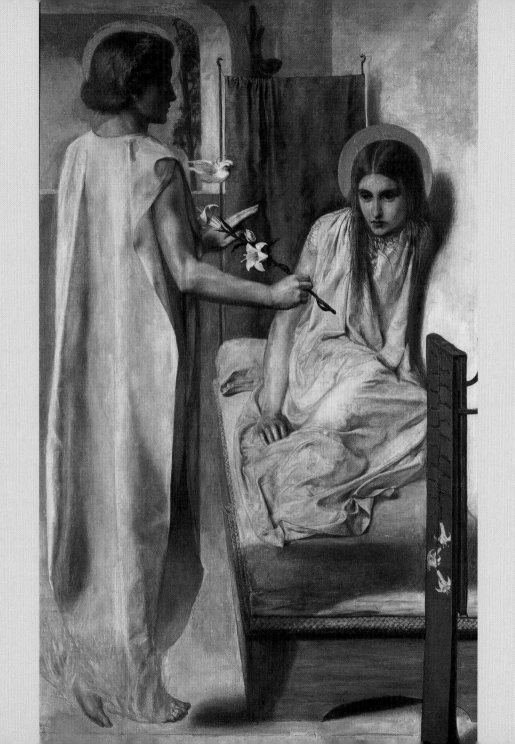

beyond their limits. Somewhere, sometime, somehow, fulfilment would come. Their dreams were not delusions but valid aspirations. It was only a matter of time.

Standing in the midst of this raging sea of anticipation and speculation, Christian writers proclaimed that the hopes of the centuries had indeed been fulfilled. The coming of Christ brought to perfection and completion the great aspirations of the seemingly endless human quest for truth. Greek philosophy and the law of Israel alike were fulfilled and transcended in this one individual, Jesus of Nazareth. Human wisdom and divine promise converged. And the point at which they converge is not an abstract idea, but the 'mathematical point' (Martin Luther) of Jesus Christ.

John Wesley caught this sense of expectation in his famous hymn 'Come, Thou long-expected Jesus', written in 1744. The hopes of Jew and Gentile, peoples and individuals, will find their fulfilment in him.

> Israel's strength and consolation,
> Hope of all the earth Thou art;
> Dear desire of every nation,
> Joy of every longing heart.

This theme is incorporated into the Church's liturgy at Advent, as Christians prepare to celebrate the birth of Christ by recalling the series of events – some glorious, some baffling, some shameful – that led to his coming. At this time, the Church recalls especially the lineage of Jesus in the history of Israel. The Christian community tries to appreciate the importance of Christ by imagining a world without him. For Christians, who have become used to breathing the oxygen of Christ that so animates their lives, this can be immensely difficult. It is like trying to think of a very different world – a world before electricity, telephones, penicillin, or cars. Yet it is only by thinking ourselves into such a situation that we can conceive the difference that Christ makes to things. By forcing us to ask about our vision of life before Christ or without Christ, we are enabled to grasp, however dimly, the transformation he brings to life and thought.

At Advent, then, the Church painstakingly traces the trajectory of God's revelation and offer of salvation to all of humanity from the creation, through the calling of Abraham, and the election of Israel as God's chosen people. It lingers with delight over the great story of Israel's deliverance from bondage in Egypt and entry into the promised land. It cherishes the promises of a yet greater redemption, in which all of humanity will be delivered from its greatest oppressors – sin and death. The same God who delivered Israel from captivity in Egypt will act again, this time to redeem all his creatures from the limits of their sinful and finite existence. But when will this happen? And in what way? And who will be the new Moses, leading a new people of God to a new promised land?

Our problem, of course, is that we already know the answer. Yet by asking precisely that question, we are forced to trace again the mysterious tracks of God in history. It is often in revisiting familiar places that we discover new insights and themes, so easily overlooked on previous occasions. As the famous bidding prayer from the Service of Nine Lessons and Carols puts it, we are invited to 'read and mark in Holy Scripture the tale of the loving purposes of God from the first days of our disobedience unto the glorious Redemption brought us by this Holy Child'.

The seven ancient 'Advent Antiphons', going back to the first Christian centuries, set out the great theme of the fulfilment of the promises of God in the coming of Christ. Each takes up a strand of expectation, weaving them into a pattern of promise and fulfilment, anticipation and achievement.

Three verses from John Mason Neale's classic translation of the Victorian era set the scene with admirable clarity:

O Come, O come, Emmanuel
And ransom captive Israel
That mourns in lonely exile here
Until the Son of God appear.
Rejoice! Rejoice! Emmanuel shall come to thee, O Israel.

O Come, Thou Key of David, come
And open wide our heavenly home;
Make safe the way that leads on high,
That we no more have cause to sigh.
Rejoice! Rejoice! Emmanuel shall come to thee, O Israel.

O Come, Thou Dayspring from on High
And cheer us by Thy drawing nigh.
Disperse the gloomy clouds of night
And death's dark shadow put to flight.
Rejoice! Rejoice! Emmanuel shall come to thee, O Israel.

The theme of the fulfilment of God's promises to Israel plays an especially significant role in Luke's Gospel, the first chapters of which focus on the two women – Elizabeth and Mary – who will play such an important part in the realization of God's purposes. Gabriel's declaration to Mary that she is to bear the Saviour of the world – a scene usually referred to as the 'annunciation' – affirms the continuity of the Gospel with the law, the Church with Israel. It is often pointed out, for example, that the 'Song of Mary' (Luke 1.46–55) echoes many of the themes of the song of an Old Testament heroine, Hannah (1 Samuel 2.1–10), as she exults in the news that she, too, is to bear a son – Samuel – for whom God has a special place in the salvation of the world.

Unsurprisingly, this scene has proved immensely popular with Christian artists. In the period of the Renaissance, Mary is often depicted as a noble lady, dressed in golden finery, humbly accepting the great responsibility placed upon her shoulders. Gabriel is generally portrayed as carrying a lily, long accepted as a symbol of purity. Yet too often, the essential humanity of the situation seems to be missing. It was as if the sheer surprise, even shock, of the angelical announcement could be ignored or overlooked. No such criticism can be directed against Dante Gabriel Rossetti's famous painting *Ecce Ancilla Domini* (Behold the handmaid of the Lord), which was first exhibited in 1850.

The work caused something of a stir, not least on account of the manner in which Rossetti portrayed Mary. Mary – here modelled by Rossetti's sister, Christina – is depicted as a young woman in a state of fear, cowering against a wall, with her eyes cast down, almost in dread. Mary, we are told, was 'greatly troubled' by Gabriel's greeting (Luke 1.29). Rossetti captures her state of mind beautifully. What he depicts is far from the humble acceptance of the noble Marys of Renaissance annunciations. If anything, Rossetti's Mary seems to be trying to get as far away from Gabriel as the small, everyday bedroom allows. The tension of the work is accentuated by its shape: its tall, narrow frame focuses attention on its central figures. There is nothing of the sumptuous gold cloth and exquisite ornamental buildings of Renaissance annunciations; Rossetti sets the scene in a small, slightly shabby, Victorian bedroom.

'How can this be?' Rossetti's vivid depiction of the scene conveys Mary's astonishment, located somewhere between dismay and fear, at the news that Gabriel brings. Her eyes seem fixed on the lily – symbolizing purity – that he holds, perhaps sharpening the question: how can I, a virgin, be about to bear *any* child – let alone the 'Son of the Most High' and successor to David? Rossetti subtly emphasizes the purity motif by allowing white to dominate the painting. Only small areas of blue, red and yellow are to be seen.

Rossetti's dramatic portrayal of fear echoes a fundamental biblical theme – that experiencing or encountering God evokes a sense of awe and overwhelming anxiety. When the women discover the empty tomb of Christ on the first Easter morning, their immediate reaction is not one of joy at the restoration of the crucified Christ, but fear – fear at the unknown, similar to Rudolf Otto's famous notion of the *mysterium tremendum*.

Again, when the shepherds, watching their flocks in fields near Bethlehem, see the glory of the Lord around them, their immediate response is fear (Luke 2.8–9). Something awesome has happened. Glory, if it is truly glory, causes us to be terrified, and at a loss for words to describe it. Gabriel's declaration to Mary leaves her shocked and astonished in about equal measure. The great theme of the fulfilment of divine prophecy suddenly ceases to be an abstract idea, and becomes something particular and specific that will transform her life and – through her obedience – the life of the world.

Lord, help us to share Mary's sense of awe and amazement in sharing in your redemptive purposes for your world. May we too be obedient to your will, whatever it may be.

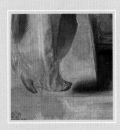

the birth of the Saviour

The story of the nativity of Jesus is perhaps the most celebrated account of any birth in human history. Christians remind themselves of this great event every Christmas, its every detail accentuated by the images of more traditional Christmas cards and the words of the great carols. The great biblical theme of the fulfilment of prophecy once more saturates the biblical narrative, as the birth of Christ is shown to continue and extend the story of God's dealings with Israel. The God of Israel has indeed visited and redeemed his people. Yet that same God has also *redefined* his people, breaking down every barrier of race, gender and status in order that all might know God's love and share in God's salvation. All are invited to feast at his sumptuous table.

The New Testament sees Jesus Christ as fulfilling the great hopes and expectations of the Old Testament. The promises made by God to Israel were brought to completion, and extended to all nations, through the life, death and resurrection of Jesus Christ. Thus the Gospel of Matthew sets out some reasons why we should draw the conclusion that Jesus was the Messiah, the long-awaited descendant of King David who was expected to usher in a new era in the history of Israel. The Gospel opens with a list of Jesus' forebears (Matthew 1.1–17) which establishes that Jesus was legally the son of David – as the Messiah was expected to be. In his account of the birth of Jesus, Matthew draws his readers' attention to the remarkable parallels between the circumstances of that birth and the prophecies of the Old Testament, making this point no fewer than five times in his first two chapters (Matthew 1.22–23; 2.5–7; 2.16; 2.17–18; 2.23).

Mark's Gospel opens by focusing our attention on the figure of John the Baptist. John is the long-expected messenger who prepares the way for the coming of the Lord (Mark 1.2–3). Having established this, Mark records John the Baptist's statement that someone even more significant will come

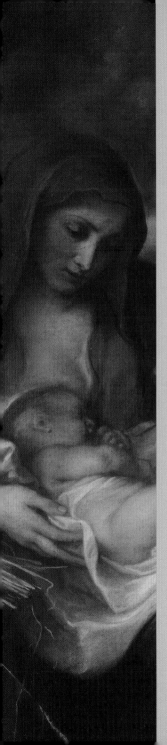

after him (Mark 1.7–8). And who is it who comes on to the scene at once? 'In those days, Jesus came from Nazareth in Galilee, and was baptized by John in the Jordan' (Mark 1.9). The astonishing conclusion that Mark wishes us to draw is obvious; it is, nonetheless, remarkable in its boldness. The Lord God of Israel has finally come? And in this person, Jesus of Nazareth? Yet this is precisely the bold, unfashionable and defiant conclusion of the New Testament.

The nativity of Christ has long played a central role in Christian iconography. Christians have always appreciated the theological and spiritual importance of the birth of the Saviour, and have found picturing this event to be helpful to personal and corporate devotion. Incarnation is about God coming 'in the flesh' – as one who bears our nature as his burden and responsibility in order that it might become healed through his loving touch. The incarnation is about the fleshing out of the grace of God – God's descent into this world of sin, so that he might raise us up to the heavenly places. John Henry Newman put this point well in the great hymn of the 'Angelicals', part of his *Dream of Gerontius*, but familiar to congregations across the world as 'Praise to the Holiest in the height':

> And that a higher gift than grace
> Should flesh and blood refine,
> God's Presence and His very Self,
> And Essence all divine.

The image of a vulnerable child has always served to emphasize the humility of God, both in entering this world in the first place, and in such a menial situation in the second. For Christian artists, the point is simple: the more we trust that God really did enter into our history as one of us, the more we can

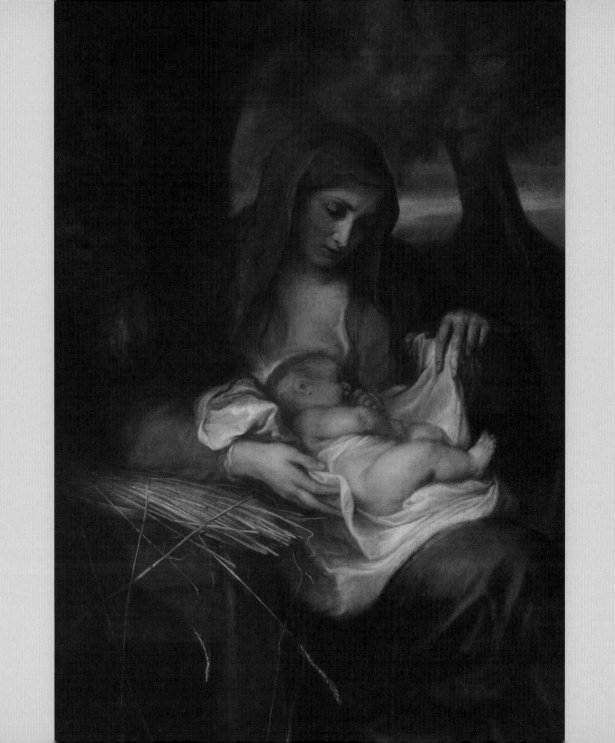

be reassured that we shall finally be raised up into those heavenly places in which the Christ-child now reigns in glory.

In the West, the dominant approach to depicting the nativity is to set Mary and her child at the centre of the picture. If the word became flesh in Christ (John 1.18), then this event – both as an idea and an image – must be the object of our contemplation. In his remarkable *Nativity*, Anthony Van Dyck (1599–1641) focuses our attention exclusively on mother and child, suggesting – but only suggesting – the context in which they are set. Mary's right arm rests on a straw-filled manger. We cannot help but notice that the straw is coarse and rough. Van Dyck wants us to be in no doubt of the lowly circumstances of Christ's birth. Yet there is a sense of stillness, of tranquillity, about the image – perhaps reminiscent of the medieval English poem so often cited in Christmas celebrations:

> He came al so stille
> There his moder was,
> As dew in Aprille
> That falleth on the grass.

In some depictions of the nativity, the themes of Christmas and Epiphany are merged. For example, in Rembrandt's *Shepherds Worshipping the Child*, we see the first visitors to the newborn king – the shepherds from the fields around Bethlehem, with some of their sheep. These are sometimes joined by the three 'wise men' from the East, who brought the newborn child the costly gifts of gold, frankincense, and myrrh. It is assumed that each 'wise man' brought one of the gifts (the Gospels do not tell us how many 'wise men' came). But Van Dyck portrays Mary and her child as solitary and unattended. Visitors may have come; but they did not linger.

Yet Mary and the infant Jesus are not totally alone. Most artists follow a long-standing tradition in including an ox and an ass in the nativity scene. Van Dyck limits himself to an ass, waiting patiently in the shadows. Yet a quick reading of the Gospel nativity accounts soon discloses that no mention is made of oxen or asses. So why are these traditionally included in the scene? From the second century onwards, commentators on the birth of Christ linked the scene with Isaiah 1.3, which speaks of the ox and the ass knowing their true master and his crib. It seems that this prophetic passage was then linked with the birth of Christ, thus reminding us that the whole of the created order is involved in the birth of Christ and the new creation which will result from his incarnation, death and resurrection. The only witnesses to the birth of Christ were the animals who were temporarily deprived of their feeding trough so that Christ might use it as his crib. Yet their witness can be seen as the created order tacitly acknowledging that their creator has entered his own domain to begin the vast work of recreation and renewal from within.

Yes, human history has many great figures – politicians, social reformers, religious teachers, and artists. And yes, all were once born. Yet their birth is little more than the biological and sociological preliminaries to what came later. It is certainly true that some interpret Christmas in basically secular terms – for example, as a reminder that we were all young once, or as a convenient illustration that the world's great thinkers often have lowly origins. Yet Christians see a much deeper level of meaning in the birth of Christ.

The nativity, as seen by the eye of faith, is about God choosing, out of love and compassion, to enter the dark, distant and lonely place that we call human history. Rather than summon us to meet him in the heavenly places, God chose to encounter us where we are. Yes, Christ went on from there – to heal the sick and to proclaim the good news of the kingdom. Yet his birth itself demands to be seen as an integral aspect of the gospel. This point is made beautifully by Thomas Pestell (1584–1659) in his 'Psalm for Christmas Day Morning'.

Behold the great Creator makes
Himself a house of clay,
A robe of virgin flesh He takes
Which He will wear for ay.

Hark, hark, the wise eternal Word,
Like a weak infant cries!
In form of servant is the Lord,
And God in cradle lies.

Van Dyck's tender image of the nativity can easily become the anchor point for one of the most important Christian insights, firmly grounded in Scripture. When God comes to earth, it is not in the form of an invading army, sent to batter down the secular defences of the world, as Babylonian armies broke through the walls of ancient Jerusalem to overpower its people. God comes into his world in dependency and weakness. The incarnation

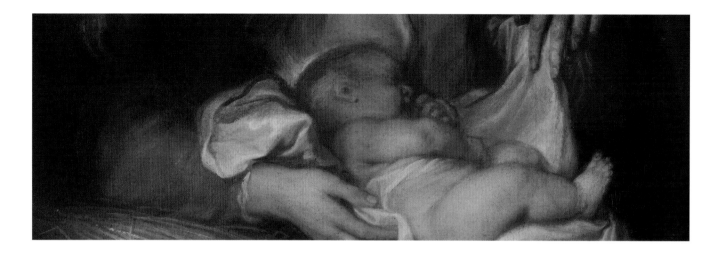

is not a destructive, aggressive act of invasion in which sinful humanity is battered into submission; it is an act of enticement in which the love of God is shown, and the love of humanity is elicited in response. God enters our world to make it known – and make it possible – that we can enter his world, not as gatecrashers or invaders but as welcome guests. God changes our world not by law or threat of force but by death and resurrection.

One of the most moving attempts to express this aspect of the theology of the incarnation is found in the poem 'New Heaven, New War' by Robert Southwell (*c.* 1561–95). Southwell writes lyrically of the overturning of human ideas of conquest and power through the birth of Christ:

> This little babe so few days old,
> Is come to rifle Satan's fold;
> All hell doth at his presence quake,
> Though he himself for cold do shake;
> For in this weak, unarmed wise,
> The gates of hell he will surprise.
> With tears he fights and wins the field,

His naked breast stands for a shield;
His battering shot are babish cries,
His arrows made of weeping eyes,
His martial ensigns cold and need,
And feeble flesh his warrior's steed.

Van Dyck's representation of the infant Christ fleshes out these ideas, enabling our imagination to engage with Southwell's astute analysis of the implications of the incarnation. Christ's weapons? Fragility and weakness. As Martin Luther emphasized time and time again, the power of God is hidden under weakness. Both the crib of Bethlehem and the cross of Calvary reveal a God who chose to be known and be active in vulnerability.

Yet there is a further feature of Van Dyck's *Nativity* that merits comment. The luminosity of the central scene immediately draws us in, focusing our attention on the infant Christ. All around him are shades and shadows. Even Mary seems to be bathed in a glow that is not her own but is reflected from Christ. Her left hand appears to be frozen in a movement – perhaps removing the swaddling clothes. Is this about the revelation of the glory of God? Is Mary's act of removing the cloth that enfolds God incarnate a metaphor for the act of divine unveiling that we call revelation?

In the theologically rich prologue to John's Gospel, we find a statement about the incarnation ('the Word became flesh, and dwelt among us') set immediately before a statement about its consequences: 'we beheld his glory' (John 1.14). This theme is traditionally linked with the season of Epiphany, in which the Church marks and recalls the revelation of the glory of Christ, and sets itself the agenda of being a bearer of that glory to the world. Historians see the Feast of the Epiphany as having its origins in the Jewish Feast of

Tabernacles, which celebrated God's glory in covenant, light and water. Epiphany is about revealing glory, and is a call to the Church to witness to and proclaim that glory to the nations.

Traditionally, the season of Epiphany is linked with the visit of the *magoi* – the 'wise men' from the East – who were drawn to worship the newborn king by the appearance of a star. They are Gentiles, drawn to seek and find their king by a natural event, not by any knowledge of prophecy. They represent the 'desire of the nations', spoken of by the prophets. Christian theology has always seen this as an anticipation of the mission to the Gentiles. The wisdom of the East led people to seek and find Christ, just as the animals are traditionally held to have recognized intuitively Christ as their Lord. Yet the real revelation of the glory of Christ takes place in his ministry itself, to which we now turn.

Lord, we thank you for choosing to come and dwell among us, as one of us. May we catch fresh glimpses of your glory – and may our own lives reflect that glory.

the calling of the disciples

the calling of the disciples

The calling of the first disciples is one of the most familiar scenes from the Gospels. A group of simple fishermen are confronted by someone whom they recognize as possessing a compelling authority – and who wants *them* to follow him. The invitation to follow is accompanied by the implication of their personal worth to him. Whoever this man is, and wherever he is going, he wants them to be with him.

> As Jesus passed along the Sea of Galilee, he saw Simon and his brother Andrew casting a net into the sea – for they were fishermen. And Jesus said to them, 'Follow me and I will make you fish for people.' And immediately they left their nets and followed him. As he went a little farther, he saw James son of Zebedee and his brother John, who were in their boat mending the nets. Immediately he called them; and they left their father Zebedee in the boat with the hired men, and followed him. (Mark 1.16–20)

Jesus called *fishermen*. Let's pause right there; the significance of this is often overlooked. Contemporary rabbinic literature had much to say about people whose jobs made them virtually incapable of keeping the law of Moses. Two groups often singled out for special (negative) comment were carpenters and fishermen: carpenters, because they doubled as undertakers and were handling dead bodies all the time; and fishermen, because they had to handle and sort mixed catches of clean and unclean fish. Both groups were incapable of observing the strict rules about ritual purity which prohibited contact with anything unclean. Yet Jesus calls precisely such fishermen, men hovering on the fringes of Jewish religious life.

The response of those fishermen was immediate and intuitive: they

left everything, and followed Jesus. No reason is given for their decision to abandon everything, and follow this stranger who has so dramatically entered into their lives. Mark leaves us with the impression of an utterly compelling figure who commands assent by his very presence. They chose to leave their nets – the basis of their meagre existence as fishermen – and follow this strange figure into the unknown. He does not even tell them his name.

Luke's account of the scene provides additional details. It becomes clear that Jesus' ministry is already under way when he encounters and calls the first disciples. A large crowd is gathering by the edge of the lake to hear him preach. Seeing two boats nearby, Jesus requests Simon to take him out into the lake a little, so that he could speak to the large crowd. After this, he asks Simon to move into deeper waters, and lower their nets. Having caught nothing all night, they are reluctant to waste time in this way. Yet the compelling character of Jesus once more asserts itself, and they do what he asks.

The scene is vividly and beautifully depicted in one of the masterpieces of late Renaissance art. Jacopo Bassano (c. 1510–92, also known as Jacopo dal Ponte) was a member of a celebrated family of artists based in the small town of Bassano del Grappo, near Venice. Bassano's *The Miraculous Draught of Fishes* (1545) is deeply influenced by aspects of Titian's major works, most notably their luxurious colours. The oil painting is scrupulously faithful to Luke's narrative. On the left, we see Simon Peter's partners in the second boat hauling in a catch of fish so great that it threatens to swamp the boat. On the right, we observe Simon Peter himself, forced to his knees in awe at what has happened. Kneeling before Jesus, he responds with a confession of his sinfulness: 'Go away from me, Lord, for I am a sinful man!' Bassano's brilliant use of colours highlights the figures in the boats, drawing our attention away from the lake in the background. The point being made is clear: the real focus of the action lies not in the sea, but in the transformation of the fishermen.

They are overwhelmed by the one who is in their midst, and can only respond with reverence and awe.

It is an immensely significant incident and demands closer scrutiny. Luke portrays the incident as a theophany – a revelation of the glory of God. It is remarkably similar to Isaiah's reaction to his vision of the glory of the Lord, seen in the temple in the year of King Uzziah's death (Isaiah 6.1–8). Isaiah's initial response to beholding the glory of the Lord is to shrink back, intensely aware of his own sinfulness – much like Simon, as portrayed by Bassano. Yet this is followed by an act of commissioning in which Isaiah, inspired and empowered by his vision of the Lord, goes forth to serve him.

> Then I heard the voice of the Lord saying, 'Whom shall I send, and who will go for us?' And I said, 'Here am I; send me!' (Isaiah 6.8)

Luke presents us with that same pattern of responding in awe to a vision of glory. Simon Peter and his colleagues are overwhelmed by what they see happening, and its implications. Initially, Simon is afraid; then he is empowered. 'When they had brought their boats to shore, they left everything and followed him' (Luke 5.11).

The scene is familiar to many churchgoers through the hymn penned by John Greenleaf Whittier (1807–92), the noted American Quaker poet who was active in the anti-slavery movement.

> In simple trust like theirs who heard,
> Beside the Syrian sea,
> The gracious calling of the Lord,
> Let us, like them, without a word,
> Rise up and follow Thee.

the calling of the disciples

This theme of a deep personal trust in Christ runs throughout the long history of Christian thought. People find in Jesus something – a reason for living, their heart's desire, a firm stronghold in times of despair, or someone who seems to know the secrets of the kingdom of God. Without fully understanding who he is, or what they find so compelling about him, they choose to follow him. Their hearts have been won. Their minds, however, must now take in what has happened. Who must Jesus be to elicit such a response on their part? What is so different about him? Their hearts led them to follow Jesus; they have yet to figure out just who he is.

This process of working out Jesus' identity is helped along by what the disciples see and hear as they follow Jesus. One incident which took place very early in the ministry of Jesus is worth thinking about here – the healing of a paralytic. Hearing that Jesus is in the vicinity, four people bring their paralysed friend to be healed by him. The crowds around Jesus' house are so great that they cannot reach him. In a stroke of genius, they decide to remove the roof of the house, and lower the paralytic inside. Thus far, the story illustrates the remarkable appeal that Jesus had to the crowds. He was someone who they knew intuitively was able to change their situations. Jesus was a healer; and people knew they needed healing.

We can see here the beginnings of an attempt to develop a Christology – an account of the identity and significance of Jesus of Nazareth. All the evidence we possess suggests that those who witnessed Jesus in action initially tried to interpret him in terms of existing models and categories – for example, as a healer or prophet. It was entirely natural to do so. After all, the Old Testament contained many references to God's way of acting in the world, and it was entirely reasonable to try and assimilate Jesus to one of these familiar patterns. So why not regard Jesus as a new Elijah, who was able to heal the sick?

Yet what happens next suggests that these attempts to assimilate Jesus to existing models simply could not do justice to his significance. We will let Mark take up the story, as he tells of how the friends lowered the paralytic to be with Jesus.

> When Jesus saw their faith, he said to the paralytic, 'Son, your sins are forgiven.' Now some of the scribes were sitting there, questioning in their hearts, 'Why does this fellow speak in this way? It is blasphemy! Who can forgive sins but God alone?' (Mark 2.5–7)

Jesus declares that the man's sins are forgiven. And when he says 'Your sins are forgiven', it sounds as if he really means it. It is an excellent example of Jesus teaching with authority. He does not say, tentatively, 'May your sins be forgiven', or 'I hope your sins will be forgiven'. When we think about it properly, this is actually a momentous claim. And what he says seems deeply subversive to the religious orthodoxy of the day. The teachers of the Jewish law who heard these words were fully aware of their implication, and wasted no time in responding. Their criticism was immediate and urgent: this man is blaspheming. It was a serious charge. If found guilty before a religious court, Jesus could be put to death by stoning.

Readers of the Gospels have become so used to disregarding the criticism directed against Jesus by the 'scribes and Pharisees' that they often forget that many of them are entirely justified. This particular criticism strikes at the heart of the question of the significance of Jesus. Rightly, the scribes point out that Jesus was claiming to be able to do something – forgive sins – that only God is able to do. And that was unquestionably blasphemy. Unless, that is, the unthinkable, the unimaginable, were to be true: unless Jesus were God. Yet that was simply inconceivable within the ways of thinking of orthodox Judaism, as the scribes correctly saw.

Yet the Gospel account of the healing of the paralytic does not end with this criticism of Jesus. It continues with Jesus responding to his critics in such a way that presses traditional ways of thinking about God's presence in the world to their absolute limits.

> 'But so that you may know that the Son of Man has authority on earth to forgive sins' – he said to the paralytic – 'I say to you, stand up, take your mat and go to your home.' And he stood up, and immediately took the mat and went out before all of them; so that

they were all amazed and glorified God, saying, 'We have never seen anything like this!' (Mark 2.10–12)

The healing of the paralytic, though important, is of secondary importance here. The amazement of the crowds arose from their realization of the implications of what they had just seen and heard. Someone had claimed authority to act as God and for God. And far from striking Jesus dead by a thunderbolt from heaven, God appeared to have honoured – even *endorsed* – this astonishing claim. What could this mean? What were its implications? And how on earth could this be accommodated within traditional ways of understanding God's presence and action within the world?

It is as if old ways of thinking fall apart when confronted with the ministry of Jesus, incapable of coping with this new disclosure. It is no accident that Mark's Gospel follows this remarkable incident with Jesus' words about the failure of old wineskins to contain new wine (Mark 2.22). The coming of Jesus into human history has introduced something new, something dynamic, that the old ways of thinking were not capable of grasping. The unthinkable was happening. And there were only two ways out of this dilemma – to deny what was happening, or to rethink the limits of divine possibilities. Might what have once been inconceivable, even blasphemous, actually have happened? And if so, what were the implications for the disciples? Just who was it that they had chosen to follow?

We can see here the beginnings of a tentative line of theological reflection, which gains momentum throughout the Gospel accounts of the ministry of Jesus. Who must this man *be*, if he is able to do *this*? For example, Mark relates how Jesus was able to still the storms on the Sea of Galilee, to the amazement of the disciples. He reports that 'they were filled with great awe, and said to one another, "Who then is this, that even the wind and sea obey him?" ' (Mark 4.35–41). The fundamental theological question is that of the relation of action and identity. In what way do these remarkable deeds of Jesus give us clues as to who he really is?

To answer this question properly, we must listen to the entire Gospel narrative of what Jesus did and said, what was done to him, and the impact that he had upon people's lives and thoughts. It is essential to engage Christ in his totality rather than in some selected aspects of his ministry. Christ is easily presented as a teacher, and only a teacher, or as a healer, and only a healer. These categories were well established. Initially, the question simply seemed to be which of these categories best suited Jesus.

Yet as the evidence mounted, it became clear that none really fitted him. Jesus conformed to existing religious categories if, and only if, significant aspects of his ministry were overlooked or ignored, or intellectual violence was used to force him to fit existing moulds. The new wine of Jesus just could not be contained by the old wineskins of existing thought patterns. Not surprisingly, they exploded under the strain, proving to be incapable of containing him. New ways of thinking were demanded by this remarkable person. The name of the new category? Incarnation.

Lord, help us to hear your call to follow you, wherever you lead us. Help us to know who you are, and what you want us to be.

the teacher with authority

The Gospels are emphatic: Jesus was a teacher – a 'rabbi', to use the traditional Jewish title. Wherever he went to teach, crowds gathered, attracted by both the substance of his teaching and the authority with which he spoke. Now the Gospel records clearly suggest that what seems to have impressed, troubled and excited the contemporaries of Jesus is that he spoke with *authority*. It was not just what he said; it was the way he said it. He seemed to speak as if authorized to communicate about God as none other.

Each of the Gospels presents the significance of Jesus' teaching in a slightly different way. Matthew's Gospel tends to present Jesus as the new Moses, delivering the new law to the new people of God. Jesus comes to fulfil the Old Testament law, not to abolish it. Luke, on the other hand, often focuses on the significance of Jesus' teaching to those outside Israel.

The Synoptic Gospels – Matthew, Mark and Luke – present Jesus' teaching primarily in terms of parables, such as the 'parables of creation' we consider in the volume *Creation*. These parables sometimes take the form of brief observations, based on the natural world or the everyday life of rural Palestine. At others, they are more elaborate, highly developed stories. For some, parables are 'earthly stories with heavenly meanings'; for others, they are better seen as extended similes and metaphors, which allow something unknown or unfamiliar to be better understood by being compared to something that is already known and familiar. The strange world of divine grace is shown to be reflected and anticipated in the everyday world, when seen in the correct way.

Perhaps one of the most decisive and distinctive features of the parables is an appeal to the human imagination, with the intention of eliciting a response. The intended response may be spiritual, practical, or ethical. The listener is invited to imagine a scene. Sometimes the scenario is sketched in outline, in the briefest of terms. Consider this familiar story:

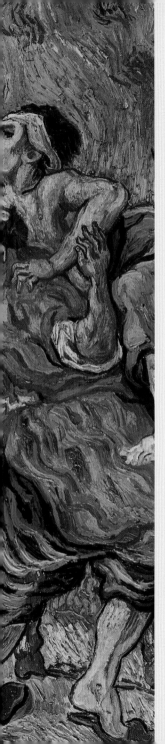

> The kingdom of heaven is like a merchant in search of fine pearls; on finding one pearl of great value, he went and sold all that he had and bought it. (Matthew 13.45–46)

Though sketched with the utmost verbal economy – a mere 25 words in the original Greek – the human imagination can easily work on this, and appreciate its power. The story rings true to experience, and proves easy to develop and apply.

Let's retell the story. A merchant finds a priceless pearl for sale, and decides that he will sell everything in order to possess it. Why? Because here is something of supreme value. Here is something which is worth possessing. Everything else he possesses seems of little value in comparison.

So what does it mean? Or, to rephrase this in a more helpful manner, what response is this meant to elicit from us? The answer seems clear. The merchant searching for that pearl is a parable of the long human search for meaning and significance. It is clear from the parable that he already possesses many small pearls. Perhaps he bought them in the hope that they would provide him with the satisfaction that he longed for. Yet when something really special comes along, he gladly sells them all in order to take hold of it.

The parable thus reminds us that many of the beliefs and values that we subscribe to are like those lesser pearls. They seemed worthwhile, and for a time offered fulfilment. Yet, deep down, we knew that there had to be something better. The accumulation of possessions does not bring happiness. Neither does the acquisition of status and power. These are like drugs with the ability to soothe and console for a while, before their potency begins to wane. We begin to look around again, seeking something which will achieve permanently what we thought these goals promised.

When the merchant found that pearl of great price, he gladly abandoned all that he had accumulated. Here, at last, was something that was worth possessing! What he had obtained previously was a preparation for this final purchase. He had come to know the true value of what he possessed, and was looking for the final culmination of his search for a precious pearl.

When the merchant saw that special pearl, he knew that everything already in his possession seemed dull and lacklustre by comparison. Just as the brilliance of the sun drowns that of the stars, so that they can only be seen at night, so this great pearl allowed the merchant to see what he already owned in a different perspective. What he had thought would satisfy him proved only to disclose his dissatisfaction, and make him long for something which was, for the moment, beyond his grasp. And then he saw that special pearl. He knew he had to have it. The parable reminds us that the gospel eclipses and overshadows its rivals, and that we must never allow them to displace it.

Other Gospel parables, however, are more complex than such simple comparisons. A good example of this more developed and elaborate type of parable is the story of the Good Samaritan (Luke 10.25–37), told by Jesus in response to the question, 'Who is my neighbour?'

A man was going down from Jerusalem to Jericho, and fell into the hands of robbers, who stripped him, beat him, and went away, leaving him half dead. Now by chance a priest was going down that road; and when he saw him, he passed by on the other side. So likewise a Levite, when he came to the place and saw him, passed by on the other side. But a Samaritan while travelling came near him; and when he saw him, he was moved with pity. He went to him and bandaged his wounds, having poured oil and wine on them. Then he put him on his own animal, brought him to an inn, and took care of him. The next day he took out two denarii, gave them to the innkeeper, and said, 'Take care of him; and when I come back, I will repay you whatever more you spend.'

It is a story that is easily visualized. One of the most famous depictions of the parable was painted by Vincent Van Gogh in May 1890. It is based on an earlier work by Delacroix in 1852, which shows the Samaritan straining to lift the wounded traveller on to his horse. Delacroix used dark colours, except for the Samaritan's robe, which is painted in a brilliant red. Van Gogh replaced Delacroix's dark palette with brilliant light hues, allowing every detail of his active brush strokes to be seen. Our attention is first claimed by the Samaritan himself, and his wounded passenger. Around them, we see a great gorge, through which a torrent of water cascades. Then our eyes stray to the left, where we see the priest and the Levite disappearing into the distance. Van Gogh does not suggest that they are running away from the wounded man. They just pass him by, without a thought, as they proceed on their journeys.

Van Gogh hints at the extent of the care which the Samaritan bestows on his patient through the box to the lower left of the painting. It is fitted with secure fastenings: its contents are precious. The story itself suggests that the box contained ointment and bandages. It now seems virtually empty, its contents having been lavished on the wounded man. The Samaritan has also relinquished his place of relative comfort and safety on his horse to the stranger. As the Samaritan raises the man, single-handedly, on to his horse, we notice his flimsy, loose sandals. The remainder of his journey over the rough, rocky terrain will not be comfortable.

So how are we to interpret this parable? Traditionally, the parable is held to affirm the compassion and love of God for all peoples, which Christians are called to reflect. For some Christian writers, every aspect of the parable is significant. An excellent example of this approach is found in Augustine of Hippo, who suggested that every detail of the narrative was rich in symbolic detail.

> The wounded man stands for Adam; Jerusalem, the heavenly city from which he has fallen; the thieves, the devil who strips Adam of his immortality and leads him to sin; the priest and Levite, the Old Testament Law and ministry which was unable to cleanse and save anyone; the good Samaritan who binds the wounds, Christ who forgives sin; oil and wine, hope and stimulus to work; the animal, the incarnation; the inn, the church; and the innkeeper, the apostle Paul.

To Augustine, the parable offered a superb framework for making sense of just about every aspect of Christian existence, including the riddle of human nature, the need for salvation, and the place of the Church in God's saving purposes.

To many modern scholars, however, this approach seems hopelessly fussy and ambitious. It is argued that the parables cannot be considered

to be highly developed allegories along the lines of John Bunyan's classic *The Pilgrim's Progress*, in which just about every point and detail in the text stands for something else. Rather, the parables are best seen as a special kind of allegory, grounded in the local situation familiar to Jesus and his audience, and aimed at eliciting a response. They are completely saturated with first-century Palestinian characters, concerns and settings.

The parables are set in the social world of farmers, fishermen, crops, fish, water, pearls, wheat, treasures, workers, landowners, masters, slaves, peasants, young maidens and (occasionally) kings. Interestingly, all these individuals are anonymous. We shall never know the name of the woman who found her coin, the shepherd who lost his sheep, or the merchant who purchased a beautiful pearl. Yet these anonymous figures have captivated the world's imagination more effectively than most named literary creations. They became the vehicles of Jesus' proclamation of the coming of the kingdom, and his teaching about the nature and purposes of God.

Yet the simple observation that Jesus taught about God raises a fundamental question. When someone speaks about God, why should we believe them? What credentials would we expect them to possess? What authorizes someone to speak about God, or for God? The Christian answer, grounded in the doctrine of the incarnation, initially seems astonishing, then appears to be arrogant, before finally being recognized as deeply satisfying: Jesus is authorized to speak of God because he *is* God.

The doctrine of the incarnation undergirds the teaching authority of Jesus. It declares that, in speaking about God, Jesus stands in a unique position – authorized by God to speak of God, while inhabiting human history. The king himself, so to speak, declares the values of the coming kingdom of God. As we have seen, one of the great New Testament themes is that the promises of the Old Testament are fulfilled in the coming of Christ. The promises made by God to his people are seen to have been honoured. But the New Testament also contains promises, made by Jesus himself on behalf of God. For example, at the heart of the proclamation of the gospel, as we find it in John's Gospel, lie the great promises of salvation: 'Anyone who believes has eternal life' (John 6.47); 'Anyone who eats my flesh and drinks my blood has eternal life, and I will raise him up on the last day' (John 6.54). According to John's Gospel, Jesus makes promises on behalf of God. He is the authorized representative of God, empowered to make such promises as God and for God.

This idea is expressed particularly well by the Hebrew idea of the *shaliach* ('plenipotentiary'). The background to this idea lies in the concept of kingship found in the ancient world, particularly the ideas of delegation and representation on the part of the king in foreign regions. When a king sent his *shaliach* to negotiate with someone, that *shaliach* was empowered to act on his behalf – to enter into agreements, to make promises, and so on. Although the king was not himself physically present in these negotiations, to all intents and purposes he might just as well have been. The promises made are made on his behalf, and will be honoured by him.

It is therefore important to notice how often we find reference in John's Gospel to the total unity of purpose of Father and Son (John 17.20–5): the Son is sent by the Father (John 6.57; 17.3), and acts on behalf of the Father (John 5.30). Jesus is clearly understood to make such promises on behalf of God, and at the desire of God, and is thus unquestionably understood as *functioning as God and for God* in this respect. Jesus functions as God's *shaliach*, his plenipotentiary representative, in whom and through whom God has pledged himself to act.

This does not mean that Jesus is merely a representative of God, or that God deals with us at second hand, by sending someone to us on his behalf, and not coming to us himself. It is simply to make a statement about one of the functions of Jesus, which needs to be seen in the light of many other affirmations about his function and identity. Jesus functions as the authorized representative of God. Yet the doctrine of the incarnation, which weaves together the New Testament witness to Jesus, leads us to conclude that he does not merely *represent* God; he *is* God. God deals with us at first hand by coming among us in Christ.

Lord, help us to treasure you in our hearts and minds as the pearl of great price, exceeding in beauty and value anything that the world can offer.

the friend of sinners

the friend of sinners

Theology both helps faith and hinders faith, in about equal measures. At its best, as Karl Barth once famously pointed out, it opens up new vistas of faith, allowing us to see the vast landscape of the Christian faith with the clarity of a Tuscan landscape on a sunlit day. It brings a new intellectual depth to our faith, and helps us forge connections with other areas of life and thought. At its worst, however, it conveys the deeply misleading idea that Christianity is simply about ideas, and that spiritual growth is measured in the accumulation of those ideas.

This misunderstanding is challenged to its very roots by one aspect of the Gospel narratives – the encounters of Jesus with individuals. All four Gospels tell us of the encounters of Jesus, and the dramatic transformation this brought to the lives of tired, confused, rejected and wounded people. Those who were rejected found acceptance; those who were wounded, healing; those who were broken were restored to wholeness.

Jesus seeks out and accepts sinners, welcoming them into his presence, in the knowledge that such a redemptive encounter must lead to personal transformation. The English poet George Herbert puts this into words in the poem with which he ends *The Temple*. In 'Love (III)' – there are two other poems entitled 'Love' in the collection – Herbert asks his readers to imagine the encounter of Love – here understood to be Jesus Christ, as God incarnate – with the believer, deeply conscious of human sin and inadequacy.

> Love bade me welcome, yet my soul drew back,
> > Guilty of dust and sin.
> But quick-ey'd Love, observing me grow slack
> > From my first entrance in,
> Drew nearer to me, sweetly questioning
> > If I lack'd anything.

'A guest,' I answer'd, 'worthy to be here';
    Love said, 'You shall be he.'
'I, the unkind, the ungrateful? ah my dear,
    I cannot look on thee.'
Love took my hand and smiling did reply,
    'Who made the eyes but I?'

'Truth, Lord, but I have marr'd them; let my shame
    Go where it doth deserve.'
'And know you not,' says Love, 'who bore the blame?'
    'My dear, then I will serve.'
'You must sit down,' says Love, 'and taste my meat.'
    So I did sit and eat.

Herbert's point is simple: Christ accepts us, knowing us for what we are, and having dealt with what we are through his cross and resurrection. We are enabled to sit and eat in his presence. For Herbert, Christ's transforming encounters with individuals embody the gospel message. Many theologians have made the point that Christ, in his personal ministry, embodies central themes of the gospel later stated in more theological terms by the apostle Paul – such as the doctrines of 'justification by faith' and 'salvation by grace'. Such doctrines risk becoming abstract ideas; in the ministry of Christ, however, they are living realities, which lead to changed lives. Indeed, we might say that, where there is no transformation of life, Christ has not really been encountered at all. He has only been seen from a distance.

An excellent example of a transformative gospel encounter is that of Zacchaeus, the tax collector (Luke 19.1–10). The Gospel account is brutally direct: despite Zacchaeus' reputation, Jesus declares that he will visit him

at his house. Not surprisingly, the crowd are astonished, and at least some of them are irritated. Is not this about the endorsement of Zacchaeus' unacceptable behaviour? No wonder that some commented that Jesus was behaving like a 'friend of sinners' – an intended insult which Jesus came to wear as a badge of honour. Surely Jesus' unconditional acceptance of sinful Zacchaeus would merely encourage sin? And insult the righteous?

It is an important gospel theme. Jesus is prepared to accept those whom his contemporaries regarded as unacceptable, beyond the limits. In what he did and what he said, Jesus seems to be redefining what it means to belong to God's people. He is acting like the God who chose Israel in the first place, redefining its boundaries and repositioning its centre. He sits at table with those whom the world regarded as outcasts, such as tax collectors, the menial puppets of the Roman authorities. He mingles with those with whom respectable people would have no dealings, such as prostitutes. He was seen alone with women – a scandalous matter at the time – and talked to them as equals about the wonders of the Kingdom of God (note the amazement of the disciples at this in John 4.27). He preached to Samaritans, to the horror of the Jews. He mingled with, spoke to, and even touched lepers, who had been cast out by society as unclean (Mark 1.40–2), risking becoming leprous himself. (There is an obvious parallel with AIDS in our own day.) He ministered to senior Roman officers, who were regarded with hatred and contempt by Jews, who saw them as oppressors. In short, Jesus was prepared to meet and accept even those whom society regarded as outcasts. But that meeting never left things as they were. Encounter leads to transformation.

This is dramatically evident in the story of Zacchaeus. Overwhelmed by being accepted by Jesus in this unexpected way, Zacchaeus repents of his former ways. 'Look, half of my possessions, Lord, I will give to the poor; and if I have defrauded anybody of anything, I will pay back four times

individual encounters of Christ stimulates our imaginations, allowing us to picture them in the theatre of our minds.

One of the reasons why representational art is so important to Christian spirituality is that it both enables and encourages this process of prayerful engagement with the Gospel narratives to take place. It helps us to visualize the location of events, and brings added realism and clarity to the exploration of the encounters of Jesus. A classic example of such an encounter is to be found in the fourth chapter of John's Gospel, which relates how Jesus encountered a Samaritan woman at a well. This has been the subject of many representations, including particularly notable works by Duccio di Buoninsegna (1308–11) and Juan de Flandes (1500). The work chosen to illustrate this chapter is, however, decidedly English.

George Richmond (1809–96) was one of the most well regarded portrait painters of the Victorian era. In his younger days, he was associated with 'the Ancients', a circle of artists which gathered around William Blake. His *Christ and the Woman of Samaria* is an early work, dating from 1828. It offers a highly distinctive rendering of the Gospel account of this meeting, focusing attention on three aspects of the narrative: the woman, the well, and Jesus himself. In the distance is the town from which the woman came to draw water; to the right is the edge of a cornfield which Jesus mentions later in the narrative.

It is a hot day, and Jesus is both tired and thirsty. Richmond's artwork suggests that the well is cool and shady, the ideal resting place from the blazing heat of the sun. Plants grow around it, refreshed by the water – a gentle hint at the way in which water renews life. As Jesus sits by the well, a Samaritan woman comes along to draw water. This encounter between Jesus and the woman is transformative at many levels. To begin with, a double prejudice is overcome: Jesus the male Jew sits and talks with the Samaritan woman. Richmond highlights the scandal of this occasion by portraying the woman as immodestly dressed by the standards of Victorian England. In this way, he recreates the sense of shock, even outrage, that this encounter would have caused within the decidedly patriarchal culture of Jesus' day.

As John's narrative progresses, we find a remarkable deepening of insight. The woman initially sees a thirsty man; finally, she recognizes him as the one who can meet her own deeper thirst for meaning and acceptance. She begins by seeing him as someone who is tired and weary, and needs refreshment; gradually, she realizes that he is the one who is able to refresh and renew others. Richmond portrays her as averting her eyes from Jesus, focusing on the jar in which she will draw water from the well. Does he want us to think of her realizing that the one whom she does not dare look upon is the ultimate source of the water of life?

The encounter thus exposes both the woman's need – here understood to mirror the situation of humanity in general – and Jesus' ability to meet it in unexpected ways. Jesus comments that anyone who drinks of the water drawn from the well will thirst again. Even that fresh water will be unable to quench the deeper thirst that lies beneath the surface of human existence.

But he is able to offer something different – a spring of living water which will both quench thirst, and bring eternal life. The deep emptiness within human nature can be satisfied by nothing that is finite or created – in other words, by God, and God alone. It is Jesus himself, and Jesus alone, who is able to slake our thirst and satisfy our deep spiritual hunger.

Yet the narrative does not end with the woman's personal response to Jesus; she wishes to share her discovery with others. She rushes back to her city to tell others of this remarkable person (John 4.28–9), so that they too might believe in him, and drink from the springs of living water that he brings. The impulse to share what we find in Jesus underlies the mission of the Church. Philip, we noted earlier, wanted Nathanael to share his delight in discovering Jesus as the culmination of Israel's hopes and aspirations. The point is simple: appreciating the riches of Christ leads to sharing them through mission and evangelism.

Lord, help us to know you – not just know about you – and to share you. Help us to discover the spring of lifegiving water that you bring to all who thirst, and refresh us with glimpses of your glory.

The Gospels tell the story of Jesus of Nazareth, each in its distinctive way. The individuality of their approaches had led scholars to try to guess whether they had a specific audience in mind. Was the way the Gospel writers assembled their material influenced by who they expected their readers to be? Matthew, for example, seems particularly concerned to stress the continuity of the Church with Israel, noting especially how Jesus came to be seen as perfecting the Jewish law, both in letter and spirit. Mark's vivid depiction of Gospel events stresses the suffering of Christ, placing particular emphasis on the prediction of his passion. Luke's Gospel has clearly been written with the interests and needs of non-Jewish readers in mind, apparently with a special concern to bring out the relevance of the 'good news' for the poor, oppressed and needy.

Yet it is important not to read too much into these differing emphases. We do not know enough about how the Gospels were compiled, or what specific sources the evangelists used, to draw secure conclusions. Perhaps the most reliable judgement is that each of the Gospels presents us with a distinctive view of Jesus, just as the biographers of modern historical figures draw out different aspects of their subject's historical and cultural importance.

John's Gospel has been the subject of much debate. Who is the intended audience for this Gospel? Who wrote this Gospel? The text of the Gospel itself indicates that its author was 'the disciple whom Jesus loved' (e.g. 13.23–36; 18.15–16). Tradition has identified this as the Apostle John, although it should be noted that the text of the Gospel itself does not make this statement explicitly. There are reasons for thinking that the Gospel may have been written with the special needs of the churches in the region of Ephesus in mind. The date of writing of the Gospel remains unclear. The Gospel text itself implies that both Peter and the 'beloved disciple' are dead

(see 21.19, 22–23), thus pointing to a date at some point after 70. This is also suggested by other factors. Most scholars suggest a date towards the end of the first century (perhaps around 85), although the possibility of an earlier date remains open.

The portrait of Jesus of Nazareth presented in John's Gospel has long been recognized as highly distinctive, complementing that found in the three Synoptic Gospels. Its opening is dramatic – 'In the beginning was the Word' – evoking the memory of the first chapter of Genesis, marking the beginning of both Christian and Jewish Bibles. Some scholars have seen John's Gospel as an extended commentary on the seven days of creation. The redemption brought by Christ suggests, recalls and evokes this sevenfold structure.

Scholars have noted how three distinct sevenfold patterns can be identified within John's Gospel. In the first place, there are seven signs through which Jesus disclosed his glory. This approach is quite distinct from that found in the Synoptic Gospels, which all tend to present the teaching of Jesus by use of miracle stories and parables in a similar way. John's Gospel includes no parables and the large number of miracles found in the Synoptic Gospels are reduced to a representative selection of seven signs, set out in John 2—11, beginning with the turning of the water into wine, and ending with the raising of Lazarus. We noted this pattern in the volume *Creation* (pages 49–58), and explored the first such sign in detail.

And what is the purpose of these signs? And why have they been recorded? John's Gospel answers these questions in the following way (John 20.30–31):

Now Jesus did many other signs in the presence of his disciples, which are not written in this book. But these are written so that you may

come to believe that Jesus is the Messiah, the Son of God, and that through believing you may have life in his name.

The passage is of particular importance as it points to selectivity on the part of the author of the Gospel. Some New Testament scholars have suggested that John chose to present only a representative selection of the 'signs' in order to make his theological points clearer. But most importantly, the passage points to the intended outcome of the signs: to believe in Jesus, and have life in his name. The Gospel is intended to elicit a response from its readers, just as the revelation of Christ's glory through the signs evoked faith in the disciples.

The second distinctive feature of John's Gospel is the use of the 'I am' sayings which have no direct parallel in the Synoptic Gospels. Each of the sayings picks up some major themes from the Old Testament (such as Israel as a vine, Moses as the giver of the bread from heaven, and God as the shepherd of Israel), and applies them directly to Jesus. The form of these sayings is grammatically unusual, making them stand out from the remainder of the text.

This point is probably a little difficult for readers not familiar with Greek to appreciate; however, the thing to note is that there is a direct similarity between the verbal form of these sayings and Exodus 3.14, in which God reveals himself to Moses as 'I am who I am'. There thus seems to be an implicit declaration of divinity on the part of Jesus within each of these sayings. The seven 'I am' sayings can be set out as follows:

6.35	The bread of life
8.12, 9.5	The light of the world
10.7, 9	The gate for the sheep

An incident in John's Gospel allows these two concerns to be explored simultaneously – the raising of Lazarus, at which Jesus speaks the words 'I am the resurrection and the life' (John 11.25). It is a Gospel scene that has delighted artists. Caravaggio's depiction of the scene (1609) is widely regarded as one of his most powerful and visionary works. *The Raising of Lazarus* (1919) by Maurice Denis (1870–1943) illustrates the imaginative appeal of this incident. In his early period, Denis was significantly influenced by Gauguin. He was a member of 'Les Nabis' – a name derived from the Hebrew word *nabi,* 'a prophet'. This post-impressionist group was active throughout the 1890s. His later works, however, are more conventional, showing clear evidence of influence by the art of the Italian Renaissance. His visits to Tuscany and Umbria in 1895 and 1897 are thought to have provoked him to review his style, and adopt a more traditional approach.

The Raising of Lazarus captures the tension of John's narrative of this famous biblical scene. Jesus stands at the centre of the picture, with the passive body of Lazarus, enfolded in grave-clothes, to our right. Symbols of mourning – most notably, women dressed in black – abound. Everyone seems to be holding their breath, waiting and wondering what will happen. One sister clutches Jesus' arm, another looks to heaven for an answer to their prayers. Perhaps Jesus has just spoken those momentous words: 'Lazarus, come out!' (John 11.43). But is this his to command? Does he have authority over death? And if so, what are the implications for his identity, and the destiny of those standing around? Denis brilliantly depicts the confluence of word and event: the fact that Jesus *is* the resurrection and the life leads to the *bestowal* of that resurrection and life. There is the closest of connections between the identity, words and deeds of Jesus.

So how does meditating on Christ as 'the true vine', 'the resurrection and the life', or the 'way, the truth and the life' help us to understand Christian beliefs about the identity of Jesus? Just as we explore the first sign of John's Gospel in some detail in the volume *Creation*, here we shall reflect on the first of the 'I am' sayings in what follows.

The first of these sayings is found at John 6.35, in which Jesus speaks the following words: 'I am the bread of life'. This immediately suggests the idea of being nourished; of meeting the specific human need of hunger. We are immediately reminded of our spiritual emptiness. We may find that we are satisfied physically, but a deeper hunger remains – a hunger for meaning, for immortality, for something that is profoundly satisfying. To speak of Christ as bread is to establish a connection with human hunger and emptiness. What humanity needs, Christ provides.

I am the bread of life. Your ancestors ate the manna in the wilderness, and they died. This is the bread that comes down from heaven, so that one may eat of it and not die. I am the living bread that came down

from heaven. Whoever eats of this bread will live for ever; and the bread that I will give for the life of the world is my flesh. (John 6.48–51)

We see here an analogy between Jesus and bread. It is not an identity; there are significant points of difference. Bread sustains us physically; it cannot sustain us spiritually, or open up the possibility of a new existence beyond the realm of the physical. Yet the 'bread of life' is rather different. As the 'bread of life', Jesus offers the hope of eternal life to those who feed on him. To know Christ is to experience this hope as a present reality, knowing that it is grounded in the trustworthiness of God.

Note also that feeding is itself an image of 'knowing Christ', affirming our need to absorb and appropriate Christ as an internal reality, rather than as a remote external figure. Some secular Roman writers suspected the early Christians of cannibalism on account of the way in which they spoke of 'feeding on Christ' or 'eating the body of Christ'. Yet the language here is that of bringing Christ into the closest of relationships with the believer. The intimacy of the relationship which Christ desires with his people is represented in the Lord's Supper, in which Christians eat bread and drink wine as a memorial of the suffering and death of Christ.

There is also a clear connection between Christ as the 'bread of life' and the great theme of 'manna' in the Old Testament accounts of the exodus from Egypt. The Lord, having led his people from captivity in Egypt, sustained them during the long period of their wanderings in the wilderness with 'bread from heaven' (Psalm 78.24; Nehemiah 9.15). God's graciousness in providing the manna finds its fulfilment in Christ, with manna being seen as an anticipation or foreshadowing of Christ himself. The true bread from heaven was not the manna in the wilderness – itself a sign, rather than the greater reality to which it pointed. We see here again one of the great themes of the New Testament: that God's gracious promises and gifts under the Old Covenant are continued and extended under the New.

The raising of Lazarus also brings out this point. In declaring that he is 'the resurrection and the life', Jesus is making a bold statement about what he personally embodies, and makes possible. As the raising of Lazarus makes clear, Jesus is the one who makes this total transformation of human existence possible. The life that he offers is not mere biological existence, stumbling along from one day to the next without purpose, joy or hope. The life that Christ brings transcends the humdrum, allowing us to begin to experience the life of heaven in the here and now. One of the most characteristic insights of John's Gospel is that eternal life begins *now*. In entering into a relationship with Christ, the believer begins something that affects us now, even though it will not reach its full perfection until heaven.

The main point to notice here is the form which these statements take. Christ is not represented as saying 'I show you the way' or 'I make it possible for you to have life', or even 'I teach you the truth'. The statements are emphatic: it is Christ himself who *is* the way, the truth and the life. He is not merely the agent through whom certain benefits are gained, wonderful though those benefits may be. He is the bread of life, who meets human hunger. The 'I am' sayings proclaim the utter inseparability of giver and gift, of person and benefit. Who Jesus *is* determines what Jesus *gives*.

This insight was brought out particularly clearly by Martin Luther. Commenting on John 14.6 – 'I am the way, the truth and the life'– Luther likened Christ to a bridge, spanning the vast chasm of sin and mortality that separate God and humanity. Luther expands Christ's words as follows:

> Make sure that you tread on me, that is, that you cling to me with a strong faith and great confidence. I will be the bridge which will carry you across. You will pass over from death and the fear of Hell into the life which awaits you. For I paved that way and path for you. I walked across it myself, so that I might take you and all my people across. All that you need to do is place your feet confidently upon me.

Luther's words are rich in biblical allusions. It is impossible to read these words without being reminded of Israel leaving Egypt through the Red Sea, or subsequently crossing the River Jordan, to enter the promised land. Luther's point is simple: Christ made himself the bridge from time to eternity, from earth to heaven, in order that we might cross over *in* him and *through* him. In Christ, God came from heaven to earth, to bring us home to dwell with him for ever.

Lord, help us to feed on you, the bread of life. May we know you as manna in our wilderness as we travel through this life, on our way to our promised land, the New Jerusalem.

incarnation: God with us

7 incarnation: God with us

'The Word became flesh and lived among us, and we have seen his glory' (John 1.14). These words form part of the preface to John's Gospel which, like the overture to an opera, introduces some of its great themes. The statement packs an immense amount of theology into a few, precise words. The Greek term *logos*, here translated as 'word', possesses a richness and complexity which the English translation fails to convey. To try and paraphrase this, we need to expand it along the following lines: 'the one who made the world has entered into the world as part of that world, and we have seen his glory'. God, having wonderfully created the world, now enters into that creation even more wonderfully, this time to recreate it, and bring it to its intended goal.

So how does God enter into this world? In what form? At what place? When? John's answer – the Christian answer – is in that little piece of human history that we call Jesus of Nazareth, who was born under the rule of Herod, and crucified under Pontius Pilate. The idea of 'incarnation' means God taking on human flesh, humbling himself to enter into human history and take on himself the entire experience of existence as a human being. He who was there from the beginning, the one who was God, became a human being in order to redeem us. As Charles Wesley's famous Christmas carol 'Hark the Herald Angels Sing!' states this point:

Veiled in flesh the Godhead see,
Hail the incarnate Deity!
Pleased as man with man to dwell,
Jesus our Emmanuel!

There was no doubt in the minds of any Gospel writer, any of the first Christian witnesses to Jesus, that he was a human being. But he was more

than that – much more than that. Jesus offered access to God, both by making God known and making God available. As part of their discipleship of the mind, Christians had to learn to 'think about Jesus as we do about God' (to quote the second letter of Clement, a late first-century Christian writing which was greatly valued by the early Church). But how was this to be expressed? How could the biblical witness to the identity and impact of Jesus be crystallized into verbal formulae? In fact, how could any form of words be good enough to do justice to this remarkable figure?

The Church was confronted with a virtually impossible task: it needed to 'freeze' the significance of Jesus, in the full knowledge that it could not really be done. How could the dynamic, charismatic person of Jesus be petrified, like a fossil of a once-living organism? How could he be frozen into words, however brave, bold and insightful they might be? The disciples, we are told, caught sight of the glory of Jesus. But how on earth was this glory to be captured? Karl Barth, widely recognized as one of the most important Christian theologians of the twentieth century, shrewdly pointed out this paradox in one of his earliest writings – his commentary on Paul's letter to the Romans. God's revelation, he argued, cannot be frozen or pinned down, any more than a bird can be stopped in mid-flight. We can never fully seize the glory of divine revelation.

We can see something of this dilemma in the account of the transfiguration (Luke 9.1–10). When Jesus is transfigured in the sight of the disciples, their initial reaction is to try and preserve this moment of glory. Could they not construct 'dwellings' or 'booths', so that this brief and dazzling display of glory might be made permanently accessible?

In one sense, this is what Christian doctrines attempt to do – preserve a mystery, even while realizing that human words can never hope to do justice to it. Yet somehow, those words help to capture that moment of

glory, allowing future generations to appreciate at least something of its wonder. Doctrines were never meant to be a substitute for Christian experience. Rather, they were meant to be a kind of 'hedge', marking out and safeguarding an area of thought about God and Christ which seemed to be faithful to Christian experience on the one hand, and Scripture on the other.

This 'hedging' process was difficult, yet it needed to be done. Jesus needed to be placed on a conceptual map. Initially, it seemed that he had to be calibrated according to the coordinates of humanity and divinity, time and eternity. (Later, of course, it was realized that *they* needed to be recalibrated according to *him* – but that is another story.) This raised the most difficult of theological questions, which the Christian Church rightly chose to wrestle with over many years, ensuring that every possible avenue of explanation, every conceivable way of representing this insight, had been evaluated. Many of the models initially evaluated were borrowed from Judaism or Greek philosophy. Might Jesus be some kind of prophet, with an especially significant endowment of the Holy Spirit? Might Jesus be a theophany – a temporary revelation of God? Or a philosophical ideal, made known under the limiting conditions of history?

The patristic period witnessed exhaustive discussion of many possible ways of conceiving Jesus' identity. One neat solution that some early Christians found attractive was to think of Jesus as God's deputy. God was too busy to do everything, so he delegated the rather troublesome business of saving the world to an underling. It made sense to some at the time, especially as Judaism had already developed the idea that God delegated some of his powers for practical purposes to some kind of archangel or intermediate.

It was neat, but it just wasn't good enough. It didn't really capture the sense of excitement that we can see in the Gospel narratives. Nor did it do intellectual justice to the rich tapestry of witness to the words, deeds and impact of Jesus on those around him. Steeped in the knowledge of God's dealings with Israel, they recognized that something new had happened – something that just didn't fit the settled patterns of existing ways of thinking. The new wine of Jesus could not be contained by the old wineskins of existing thought patterns. Not surprisingly, they exploded under the strain. They were incapable of containing him. New ways of thinking were demanded by this remarkable person.

By the end of the fourth century, the Church had made up its collective mind, and decided that the only acceptable way of describing Jesus of Nazareth was using what has come to be known as the 'two natures' formula – namely, that Jesus is 'truly divine and truly human'. This is often referred to as the 'Chalcedonian definition', as it was fully set out by the Council of Chalcedon in 451.

Some have argued that this represents a move away from the simplicity of the biblical witness towards a more metaphysical view of Jesus, and suggested that this is an illegitimate and unnecessary development. The Church, they suggest, wandered off into the badlands of Greek metaphysics, or was seduced into transferring the attributes of power, dignity and prestige of Roman emperors to Jesus. Whether the Church got caught up in pointless metaphysical speculation or the corrupting dynamics of imperial power, it was argued, the outcome was the same: the simple New Testament vision of Jesus gets lost.

Let's just pause here. The *simple* New Testament vision? The point here is that that vision is highly complex, weaving together strands that occasionally seem to contradict each other. Here is someone claiming the prerogatives of God – such as the right to forgive sin – who is so totally obedient to God that it is inconceivable that he is trying to usurp God. Here is someone who is clearly human – who gets tired, thirsty, and so on – but who says and does things that put him way beyond humanity, on any understanding of an index of its capacities. It's not a 'simple' picture, and cannot lead to a 'simple' answer. In this case, 'simple' just means simplistic – failing to attend to the complexity of the issues.

So did the Christian desire to make Christ into the real governor of the universe really lead to him being represented as a glorified emperor? We can explore this question by looking at one of the most famous Byzantine images of Christ – a mural in the great church of Hagia Sophia ('Holy Wisdom') in what is now the Turkish city of Istanbul, but was formerly the great Christian city of Constantinople. It is a beautiful image, typical of the golden age of Byzantine religious imagery. There is no commentary, other than the abbreviation for the Greek words for 'Jesus Christ' on either side of the image.

Now even the most cursory examination of this famous image shows that the 'Jesus as glorified Roman emperor' argument has some serious problems. For a start, Jesus is generally pictured – as here –with long hair and a beard, something quite alien to traditional ways of picturing Roman emperors. He is clearly represented as someone who is outside the establishment, not part of it. Furthermore, Jesus is not depicted as wearing

imperial clothes. He is dressed as a wandering teacher, wearing an ordinary tunic and shawl. Traditional secular images of Roman emperors from this period often represent them as wearing military dress. Yet Christ is dressed as a commoner, not a noble; and as a teacher, not as a warrior. He holds a book, not a sword, nor any symbol of power or authority.

The real point being made by these Byzantine images of Christ is that a wandering Galilean peasant teacher has to be recognized as enthroned on high as 'ruler over all (*pantokrator*)'. The splendid image from Hagia Sophia makes the point that someone whom the world regarded as lowly and insignificant has now been raised to glory. The paradox of the incarnation is that God chose to subvert human preconceptions of authority by raising to the highest place one who was regarded as utterly inconsequential and insignificant by the authorities of his day. The incarnation is about the overthrow, even the inversion, of human values – not their endorsement.

So what difference does this doctrine of the incarnation make? What insights does it allow? How does it impact on our prayer? Our worship? Perhaps the simplest answer is this: it means that *God is Christ-like*. When Christians speak about God, they mean God as he has been revealed in

Jesus Christ, the God who became incarnate. The great Scottish theologian Hugh Ross Mackintosh expressed the central place of the incarnation in the following way:

> When we come to know God in the face of Jesus Christ, we know that we have not seen that Face elsewhere, and could not see it elsehow. Christ is the Way, the Truth and the Life, and there is no door, nor way, leading to the Father but by him.

Jesus is like an authorized visual aid to understanding God, capable of disclosing God to us – *disclosing God*, because he is God, and *to us*, because he entered into our midst and dwelt among us, allowing us to behold his glory. He is someone who is empowered to allow us to know what God is like. 'Anyone who has seen me has seen the Father' (John 14.9). Dorothy L. Sayers, the celebrated writer of crime fiction with a passion for theology, summed up the importance of the doctrine like this in a lecture given during the Second World War:

> The central dogma of the Incarnation is that by which relevance stands or falls. If Christ was only man, then He is entirely irrelevant to any thought about God; if He is only God, then He is entirely irrelevant to any experience of human life.

Jesus thus offers access to God, making God *known* and making God *available*. The gospel offers not merely communication with God but communion in God.

It is a theme that has been explored to the full in Christian theology. John Calvin argued that Jesus Christ is the mediator between God and humanity (picking up the imagery of Hebrews 9.15 and 1 Timothy 2.5). He is to be seen as the unique channel or focus through which God's redeeming work is directed and made available to humanity. Since it was impossible for us to ascend to God, on account of our sin and limits as human beings, God chose to descend to us instead. Unless Jesus Christ was himself a human being, other human beings could not benefit from his presence or activity. As Calvin puts it: 'The Son of God became the Son of Man, and received what is ours in such a way that he transferred to us what is his, making that which is his by nature to become ours through grace.'

Calvin's stress upon the mediatorial presence of God in Christ leads him to insist upon a close connection between the person and the work of Christ. Drawing on a tradition going back to Eusebius of Caesarea, Calvin argues that Christ's work may be summarized under three offices or ministries – prophet, priest, and king. Jesus brings together in his person the three great mediatorial offices of the Old Testament. In his *prophetic* office, Jesus is the herald and witness of God's grace. In his *kingly* office, Jesus has inaugurated a kingship which is heavenly, not earthly; spiritual, not physical. Finally, through his *priestly* office, Jesus is able to restore us to divine favour, through offering his death as a satisfaction for our sin.

And with that, Calvin reminds us that there is an integral connection between incarnation and redemption – between the person and the work of Christ. In the volume *Redemption*, this matter is explored in greater detail.

Lord, we thank you that you entered and dwelt in our world, to bring us home to heaven. We pray that you would keep this hope alive in our minds, hearts and imaginations.

for further reading

Introductory

The following are suitable for those engaging with scholarly discussion of the identity of Jesus of Nazareth for the first time.

Brown, Raymond E., *An Introduction to New Testament Christology*. New York: Paulist Press, 1994.

McGrath, Alister E., *Christian Theology: An Introduction*. 3rd edn. Oxford/ Cambridge, Mass.: Blackwell Publishers, 2001.

O'Collins, Gerald, *Christology: A Biblical, Historical and Systematic Study of Jesus*. Oxford: Oxford University Press, 1995.

More advanced

Barton, Stephen C., *The Spirituality of the Gospels*. London: SPCK, 1992.

Bauckham, Richard, *God Crucified: Monotheism and Christology in the New Testament*. Grand Rapids: Eerdmans, 1999.

Borg, Marcus J. and N. T. Wright, T*he Meaning of Jesus: Two Visions*. London: SPCK, 1999.

Bornkamm, Günther, *Jesus of Nazareth*. New York: Harper, 1960.

Capon, Robert Farrar, *Kingdom, Grace, Judgment: Paradox, Outrage, and Vindication in the Parables of Jesus*. Grand Rapids: Eerdmans, 2002.

Clark, Stephen B., *Redeemer: Understanding the Meaning of the Life, Death and Resurrection of Jesus Christ*. Ann Arbor: Servant Publications, 1992.

Dunn, James D. G., *Christology in the Making: A New Testament Inquiry into the Origins of the Doctrine of the Incarnation*. 2nd edn. Grand Rapids: Eerdmans, 1996.

Dunn, James D. G, *Jesus Remembered*. Grand Rapids: Eerdmans, 2003.

Fredriksen, Paula, *From Jesus to Christ: the Origin of the New Testament Images of Jesus*. New Haven: Yale University Press, 1988.

Grant, Robert M., *Jesus after the Gospels: The Christ of the Second Century*. Louisville: Westminster John Knox Press, 1990.

Hultgren, Arland J., *Christ and His Benefits: Christology and Redemption in the New Testament*. Philadelphia: Fortress Press, 1987.

Hultgren, Arland J., *The Parables of Jesus: A Commentary*. Grand Rapids: Eerdmans, 2002.

Hurtado, Larry W., *Lord Jesus Christ: Devotion to Jesus in the New Testament*. Grand Rapids: Eerdmans, 2003.

Johnson, Elizabeth A., *Consider Jesus: Waves of Renewal in Christology*. New York: Herder & Herder, 1992.

Johnson, Luke Timothy, *The Real Jesus: The Misguided Quest for the Historical Jesus and the Truth of the Traditional Gospels*. San Francisco: HarperCollins, 1995.

Kelly, J. N. D., *Early Christian Doctrines*. Revised edn. San Francisco: Harper & Row, 1978.

Macquarrie, John, *Jesus Christ in Modern Thought*. London: SCM Press, 1990.

Marshall, I. Howard, *The Origins of New Testament Christology*. Downers Grove, Ill.: InterVarsity Press, 1990.

Moltmann, Jürgen, *Jesus Christ for Today's World*. Minneapolis: Fortress Press, 1994.

Morris, Thomas V., *The Logic of God Incarnate*. Ithaca, NY: Cornell University Press, 1986.

Moule, C. F. D., *The Origin of Christology*. Cambridge: Cambridge University Press, 1977.

Stibbe, Mark W. G., *John as Storyteller: Narrative Criticism and the Fourth Gospel*. Cambridge: Cambridge University Press, 1992.

Theissen, Gerd, *The Shadow of the Galilean: The Quest of the Historical Jesus in Narrative Form*. London: SCM Press/Fortress Press, 2001.

Witherington, Ben, *The Christology of Jesus*. Minneapolis: Fortress Press, 1990.

Wright, N. T., *Jesus and the Victory of God*. London: SPCK/Fortress Press, 1996.

Wright, N. T., *The Challenge of Jesus*. London: SPCK/InterVarsity, 2000.

Young, Frances, *From Nicaea to Chalcedon*. London: SCM Press, 1983.

illustrations

Ecce Ancilla Domini (The Annunciation), 1849-50 (oil on canvas) by Dante Gabriel Rossetti (1828–82), Tate Gallery, London.

Nativity by Anthony Van Dyck (1599–1641), Galleria Nazionale d'Arte Antica, Rome, © 1990, Photo Scala, Florence – courtesy of the Ministero per i Beni e le Attività Culturali.

The Miraculous Draught of Fishes, 1545 (oil on canvas) by Jacopo Bassano (*c.* 1515–92), Patrons' Permanent Fund, Image © 2004 Board of Trustees, National Gallery of Art, Washington DC.

The Good Samaritan (after Delacroix), 1890 (oil on canvas) by Vincent Van Gogh (1853–90), Collection State Museum Kröller-Müller, Otterlo, The Netherlands.

Christ and the Woman of Samaria, 1828 (tempera on wood) by George Richmond (1809–96), Tate Gallery, London.

The Raising of Lazarus, 1919 (oil on canvas) by Maurice Denis (1870–1943), Private Collection/Bridgeman Art Gallery.

Mosaic depicting the Deesis Christ, South Gallery, Byzantine, 14th century (mosaics), Hagia Sophia, Istanbul, Turkey/Bridgeman Art Library.